Light All Around Us

How Do We Use Light?

Daniel Nunn

www.raintreepublishers.co.uk
Visit our website to find out more information about Raintree books.

To order:

☎ Phone 0845 6044371

📄 Fax +44 (0) 1865 312263

✉ Email myorders@raintreepublishers.co.uk

Customers from outside the UK please telephone +44 1865 312262

Raintree is an imprint of Capstone Global Library Limited, a company incorporated in England and Wales having its registered office at 7 Pilgrim Street, London, EC4V 6LB – Registered company number: 6695582

Text © Capstone Global Library Limited 2013
First published in hardback in 2013
The moral rights of the proprietor have been asserted.

Edited by Dan Nunn, Rebecca Rissman, and Siân Smith
Designed by Marcus Bell
Picture research by Tracy Cummins
Production by Victoria Fitzgerald
Originated by Capstone Global Library Ltd
Printed and bound in China by South China Printing Company Ltd

ISBN 978 1 406 23814 3 (hardback)
16 15 14 13 12
10 9 8 7 6 5 4 3 2 1

British Library Cataloguing in Publication Data
Nunn, Daniel.
   How do we use light. -- (Light all around us)
   1. Light--Juvenile literature.
   I. Title II. Series
   535-dc23

Acknowledgements
The author and publisher are grateful to the following for permission to reproduce copyright material: Corbis p.7 (© Ansgar Photography); Getty Images pp.5 (Uwe Krejci), 6 (Radius Images), 9 (Konradlew), 10 (Jan Greune), 13 (Stockbyte), 14 (Anthony Plummer), 15 (James Smith), 17 (Takashi Kitajima), 19 (Jorg Greuel), 21 (Blend Images/Ariel Skelley), 23b (Stockbyte); istockphoto p.16 (© Michal Maryniak); Shutterstock pp.4 (© MalDix), 8 (© Olegusk), 11 (© laurent dambies), 12 (© manfredxy), 18 (© Lucian Coman), 20 (© manzrussali), 22a (© dedi), 22b (© Nickolay Khoroshkov), 22c (© oneo), 23c (© manfredxy), 23d (© Olegusk).

Cover photograph of Sydney Light show reproduced with permission of Corbis (Martin Jean-Dominique). Back cover photograph of solar panels reproduced with permission of Shutterstock (manfredxy).

We would like to thank David Harrison, Nancy Harris, Dee Reid, and Diana Bentley for their assistance in the preparation of this book.

Every effort has been made to contact copyright holders of material reproduced in this book. Any omissions will be rectified in subsequent printings if notice is given to the publisher.

Contents

What is light?

Light stops things from being dark.

Light lets us see things with our eyes.

Light bounces off things and passes into our eyes.

This is how we can see things.

Some light comes from the Sun.

Some light is made by people.

How do we use sunlight?

People use sunlight to see.

Plants use sunlight to make food.

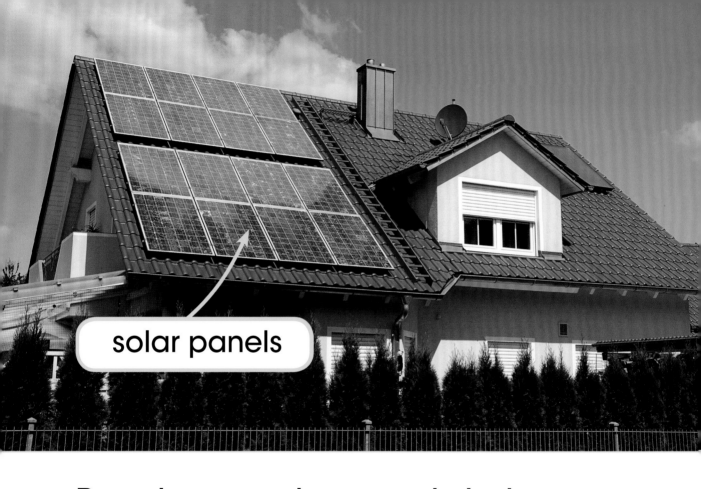

solar panels

People use solar panels to turn sunlight into electricity.

solar panels

Electricity makes some machines work.

How else do we use light?

We use some light to help us see
when it is dark.

We use a torch to help us see when
it is dark.

We use some light for decorations.

We use fairy lights for decorations.

We use some light to tell us
information.

18

We use traffic lights to tell us when to
stop and go.

We use some light for fun.

We use light from computer screens
to see pictures.

Using light quiz

a

b

c

Which light is used by plants to make food?

Answer on page 24

Picture glossary

dark when there is no light

electricity a form of energy that makes machines work

solar panel a machine that turns rays from the Sun into electricity

Sun the star closest to Earth

Index

Answer to question on page 22
The answer is **c**. Plants use sunlight to make food.

Notes for parents and teachers

Before reading
Talk to the children about light. Explain that light is what stops things from being dark. If possible, darken the room. Ask the children if being in the dark affects their ability to see. Ask them how they could make the room lighter, for example by opening the curtains, switching the light on, shining a torch, and so on.

After reading
Explain that we use light for different things. Can the children remember any other uses of light apart from helping us to see? Remind them that we also use light for decoration, to give us information, to generate electricity, or to make the screens work in equipment such as televisions, computers, and mobile phones. Can they find any examples of each use of light in the room they are in?